Duke Hawkins S001

Photo: Gert Trachez

Juan Carlos I

Juan Carlos Primero

When we were preparing for our book on the Harrier II, photographers Kris Christiaens and Gert Trachez had the possibility to visit the Spanish aircraft carrier Juan Carlos I. This resulted in such an impressive amount of photos that we decided to make a book specifically on the ship - and hopefully start a series of books on aircraft carriers. The Juan Carlos is a fairly new ship; it entered service with the Spanish Navy on September 30, 2010. First metal for the ship was cut in 2005 and the first block for construction was placed in July 2006. The ship is used in multipurpose operations for both Navy and Army, with the aft part of the ship being used as a dock for landing craft, transporting troops, equipment or vehicles, such as ambulances, trucks or armoured vehicles. Although the Juan Carlos I is impressive with a length of 231 meter, it is compact compared to the big American aircraft carriers. The crew of the ship is a minimum of 261 personnel: 30 officers, 49 NCOs, 59 leading seamen and 123 ratings, ensuring operations by either 8-12 Boeing AV-8B Harrier II Plus or a large fleet of helicopters. In this book, we take you on a tour around the ship, both on the flight deck and inside of it. And we bring a quick visit to Rota, the home base of the ship ànd the units flying from it.

This publication is based on the photos made by Kris Christiaaens and Gert Trachez, with material added by Antonio Mayandia, Laurent Heyligen - who visited Rota in 2018 - and Sergio Ruiz Gonzalez and Luis Diaz-Bedia Astor. We hope you'll enjoy this portrait of a truly impressive ship. And with some luck, we can present you more books on aircraft carriers soon!

Photo: Kris Christiaens

Special thanks to these gentlemen, all good-looking:
Kris Christiaens, Gert Trachez, Antonio Mayandia, Luis Diaz-Bedia Astor, Laurent Heyligen, Sergio Ruiz Gonzalez, Fuerzas Armadas Españolas and Gunter Geens.

Juan Carlos Primero

Photo: Kris Christiaens

Introduction

The 27,000 tons ship was built in the Navantia Shipyards in Galicia between 2005 and 2008, after which trials began for the commission. It took nearly 4 million hours of engineering and production to build the ship. It has a range of some 17,000 km - 9,000 nautical miles - and can navigate at speeds of up to 21 knots, which is about 40 km/h. The design and concept of the Juan Carlos I proved to be quite successful, since two more have been built for the Australian Navy, with those ships being named HMAS Canberra and HMAS Adelaide, although these only operate helicopters. Turkey is building a modified version of the ship as well, the TCG Anadolu, which the country hopes to have ready by 2021.

This photographical portrait of the ship has been diveded into the chapters below, with obviously a large part of the spotlights going to the EAV-8B Harrier II Plus, which has been dubbed Matador II in Spain. Let's go!

Juan Carlos Primero Introduction	06
The crew of the Juan Carlos I	10
EAV-8B Harrier II Plus	18
A look around the flight deck	42
Helicopter operations	52
Amphibious Operations	66
A closer look at the ship	74
Protecting the ship	90
Back on land	92
Rota's maintenance hangar	100

Photo: Kris Christiaens

Airborne capacity at sea

The Juan Carlos I is an amphibious aircraft carrier and the largest ever built in Spain. Her NATO denomination is Landing Helicopter Deck - LHD - but the ship also operates the fixed wing EAV-8B Harrier II Plus. The aircraft, which has VTOL capabilities- Vertical Take Off & Landing - lands vertically on the deck and uses the 12 degree ski-jump ramp to get airborne. Usually, the aircraft are parked and chained on the flight deck, but they can also be stowed in the large hangar underneath the deck. The Harrier brings the capability of a serious punch to the ship, both air-to- air, air-to-ground or air-to-sea.
Below: An EAV-8B has just landed on the aft deck and is being directed towards a parking spot on the deck by an aircraft handler.

Photo: Gert Trachez

Photo: Gert Trachez

Above: The commander of the ship during our visit was Capitan Francisco José Asensi Pérez, who sits in the forward position in the command room, facing the bow of the Juan Carlos I, with the flight deck to the left, binoculars at the ready for anything appearing on the horizon.

Photo: Kris Christiaens

Photo: Gert Trachez

Above: A trio of Harrier II Plus jump jets sit on the deck of the Juan Carlos I, aft of the super structure. Notice how the compact fighter jets are secured near the edge of the flight deck. The Harrier has 6 underwing pylons, of which 4 are wet - capable of carrying additional fuel tanks. Right: An LCM-1E landing craft is leaving the flooded part of the ship for an amphibious training excercise, loaded with an ambulance and a Mowag Piranha IIIC armoured fighting vehicle.

Photo: Kris Christiaens

Versatile helicopters are used extensively on the Juan Carlos I, like this Sea King, about to land on the aft part of the flight deck. This was one of a pair of Sea Kings, which, during an excercise brought heavily armed Spanish Marines onto the ship.

Right: The Spanish version of the Harrier is based on the radar-equipped AV-8B Harrier II Plus. At the heart of this version of the jump jet is the Pegasus Mk.107 engine. These Harriers form the offensive part of the Juan Carlos I. This photo shows a pilot entering his jet for a training mission. The boarding steps are located on the starboard side of the aircraft, with one step lowered from the air intake. Notice the detonation cord on the canopy and the HUD - Head Up Display - underneath the windscreen.

Photo: Gert Trachez

Pilots & crew of the fleet

One of the first things we witnessed on board of the ship, before the Harriers and helicopters came in for landing, was the FOD walk. FOD - Foreign Object Damage - is a huge hazard on aircraft carriers. During the FOD walk, a large number of crew gather on top on the ski-jump, form a line and slowly walks to the aft of the flight deck. Any object, even the smallest one, is picked up to prevent it from being sucked up into the jet intakes of helicopters or Harriers.

Photo: Gert Trachez

The crew of the Juan Carlos I

Photo: Kris Christiaens

The most important part of the ship is the crew. The crew consists of at least 261 people: 30 officers, 49 NCOs, 59 leading seamen and 123 ratings, which is a very limited number of people to get a ship the size of the Juan Carlos I operational. Each one of them is a professional who knows exactly what is expected of him/her, from the fire fighters to the deck crew, doctors, ordnancemen, refuellers or cooks. Operations can be going on night or day, so the crew has to be trained for that as well...

Photo: Gert Trachez

Juan Carlos Primero
The Crew

Photo: Kris Christiaens

Above: For the FOD walk, everyone is working together, usually in two lines, to make sure that nothing gets by. Even the slighest item being sucked into a jet air intake can seriously damage the aircraft or even make it crash, so the FOD walk is an important part of the day. The deck crew all have a coloured vest, explaining their fucntion on the ship. Yellow is for aircraft handlers, purple for refuellers, green for crew taking care of the deck, handling cargo, ground equipment, etc.
Right: Fire fighters gather on the hangar deck, immediately below the flight deck for a briefing before a night time mission.

Photo: Kris Christiaens

Right: Crew wearing a red vest are ordnancemen, who are responsable for handling weapons. They make sure that missiles and bombs are mounted correctly on the Harrier's pylons, but also fix or remove external fuel tanks, as can be seen in this photo.

Photo: Kris Christiaens

Below: During a fire drill, all crew wear protective equipment, even on the ship's bridge, where crew are standing around large deck plans. The photo next to it shows the ship's protection crew wearing the fire equipment under their helmets.

Photo: Kris Christiaens

Photo: Kris Christiaens

Photo: Kris Christiaens

The pilot of this Harrier II and the aircraft handler signal each other on the deck. Moments later, the pilot speeds down the deck towards the ski-jump ramp for take off. Notice the exhaust, formation strips and yaw vane on the forward fuselage. The Harrier II is capable of speeds of up to Mach 0.95 and a maximum take off weight of 14,1 tons. This is when the aircraft is using the ski-jump; when the aircraft is taking off vertically, the take off weight is reduced to just 9,4 tons.

Right: Blue plane handlers show that the chains and wheel chocks are cleared from the Harrier, indicating that the pilot has control to move the jet towards the take off spot. The yellow shirted aircraft handler gives the final thumbs up. Notice that the Harrier has a pair of large fuselage fences underneath the fuselage. These ensure stability in flight. They can be replaced with gun pods, where the port pod is the gun while the starboard pod contains the ammo.

Photo: Kris Christiaens

Photo: Kris Christiaens

Left: An aircraft handler and a blue shirt plane handler are kicking and pulling the wheel chock from the nose wheel gear. The jet's engine is already running and the landing light is on. The deck crew on board the Juan Carlos I is highly trained, which is absolutely necessary, since it is a dangerous place, with all the jet engines and helicopter rotors around!

Photo: Kris Christiaens

EAV-8B Harrier II Plus

Photo: Kris Christiaens

The star of the flight deck is the EAV-8B Harrier II Plus. In this chapter, we look at the action and the details of this amazing fighter jet. The Harrier is equipped with 4 movable nozzles, giving the aircraft the possibility to take off and land vertically.

Left: This Matador II, as the Harrier II Plus is known in the Spanish Navy, is being refuelled on the deck, with the engine running - notice the turbine and the open auxiliary doors. While refuelling, the in-flight refuelling probe is extended and the pilot waits patiently. The photo above shows the limited room the cockpit provides the pilot, but as well the good all-round visibility. Notice the horizontal blade antennas on either side of the fuselage close to the air intakes. These are part of the homing system used to land on the carrier in bad weather conditions or during the night.

Photo: Kris Christiaens

Photo: Gert Trachez

Above: The pilot of this Harrier II is waiting for clearance from flight control to excellerate towards the 12 degree ski-jump ramp and take off for another training mission. The aircraft is loaded with a pair of external fuel tanks on the inner pylons, but these can also be carried on the middle pylons. Notice that the trailing edge flaps are already in the down position and the nozzles in aft position.

Left: This photo by Gert Trachez shows a feature that is specific for the EAV-8B Matador II: immediately in front of the forward nozzle fairing, a horizontal blade antenna can be found on both sides of the aircraft. The blade antennas are part of the homing system with which the Spanish Harriers are equipped, helping the pilots to land the jet on the flight deck in the dark and during bad weather conditions. Notice the underside of the LERX and the in-flight refuelling probe in this photo.

Photo: Kris Christiaens

Photo: Kris Christiaens

Above: A trio of Matadors are secured to the deck by means of many chaines and wheel chocks. Of notice is that they all carry a target pod on the centerline pylon. The Spanish Navy operates 12 of the type at the moment, which will remain in service until at least 2027. It is at the moment unclear if they will be replaced with F-35Bs. Right: This photo shows the clear view of the deck from the command room of the Juan Carlos I. Notice that the equipment fixed to the ceiling has been tagged with a couple of stickers! Units leaving their marks !

Photo: Gert Trachez

Left: This photo shows the top fuselage of the Harrier II Plus to good effect. Notice the 4 air scoops on top of the fuselage, which are also used in case of an engine fire to extinguish the internal parts. This photo also shows the size of the 100% LERX - Leading Edge Root Extension. Further up the spine is the VHF/UHF blade antenna, a navigation light and the GPS antenna, next to the water reservoir filler cap. To get more power from the engine, water can be injected in the combustion chamber, which keeps the temperature of the compressor blades down.

Below: a close-up of the nose wheel, with the tie down points and wheel chock. Notice the landing light and the smaller red-cloured taxi-light. The gear swivels just below the landing light, making it easy to move the jet around on the deck.

Photo: Gert Trach

Juan Carlos Primero
AV-8B Harrier II Plus

Photo: Gert Traeber

Photo: Kris Christiaens

Some more great shots of the Harrier II Plus tied down on the deck. On the centerline of the jet, a Litening II target pod is fixed in between the fuselage fences. This pod includes FLIR - Forward Looking Infra Red - and increases combat effectiveness at any moment of the day or in bad weather conditions for air-to-ground or air-to-sea attacks.

Left: The Harriers are fixed to the deck on the nose wheel and the outer riggers.

WARNING
CONTAINS A CARTRIDGE
EMERGENCY ESCAPE SYSTEM
WITH EXPLOSIVE CHARGES.
MAINTENANCE MANUAL
COMPLETE INSTRUCTIONS.
DANGER
EJECTION SEAT
&
CANOPY
DANGER
DANGER
PUSH

Juan Carlos Primero
AV-8B Harrier II Plus

Photo: Kris Christiaens

Photo: Gert Trachez

I so like these kind of close-up photos! You can almost feel the fuselage of the Harrier II and hear the noice of the Pegasus Mk.107! Notice all the details in this photo: the Head-Up Display, the detonation cord on the canopy ceiling, the yaw vane in front of the windscreen and the very cool reflection of the ship's super structure in the pilot's visor. Above: A Harrier II is about to land on the flight deck. Gear down, flaps down, nozzels down, landing light on. Better protect you ears!

Photo: Kris Christiaens

Photo: Kris Christiaens

Photo: Gert Trachez

Top: Throttle forward, full power! Matador 25 is blasting towards the ski-jump ramp and take off for another training mission.
Left: This photo provides a nice close-up of the aircraft's radome. Underneath it, an APG-65 radar is located, which was adopted from the F/A-18 Hornet. On top of the radome is the Forward Looking Infra Red.

Photo: Kris Christiaens

Photo: Kris Christiaens

Above and right: The same jet during it's run towards the ramp and just moments after it gets airborne. Notice the position of the large trailing edge flaps. Apart from the action, this photo is just amazing, with the sunlight reflecting on the water and the top fuselage.

Photo: Gert Trach

Above: How about this for a fly-by shot? This Harrier II Plus is carrying a GAU-12U Equaliser gun underneath the fuselage. This is a Gatling type gun with 5 barrels, firing 25 mm ammunition. The actual gun is located in the port gun pod. The starboard pod contains 300 rounds of ammunition with a bridge in between the two pods to feed the gun. The gun itself fires at a rate of 3,600 rounds a minute, so firing time is limited. Notice the RAM air intake at the base of the vertical tail; this measures the airspeed of the aircraft. Compared to the BAE Systems Harrier II, the base of the vertical tail is much longer.

Right: This frontal view shows the size of the air intakes to good effect. The pilot has powered up the Pegasus Mk.107 engine, but the jet is still chained into position.

Photo: Gert Trachez

Above: The yellow vest aircraft handler is directing the pilot of this Harrier II Plus towards the take off point. Notice the blade-shaped vent on the forward nozzle fairing; This is the oil breather for the Pegasus engine. Underneath it, near the belly of the aircraft, a larger vent can be seen. This is the fuel breather mast.

Right: A Harrier II Plus is taxiing towards a parking spot on the flight deck, next to the ski-jump, seen from inside the command post of the Juan Carlos I. The window is being used as a board to remind the commander what movements can be expected during the day. As can be seen, some Sea Kings helicopters have been announced, coming from the Galicia - L51 - and her sister ship Castilla - L52.

Photo: Kris Christiaens

Photo: Luis Diaz-Bedia Astor

Photo: Gert Trachez

Above: Late afternoon and Matador 23 is hovering next to the Juan Carlos I, ready to land on the flight deck. Notice the large trailing edge flaps in the full down position ensuring that the thrust of the aft nozzles is vectored in the right direction. This photo shows the weathering and colouring coming from the nozzles in quite a spectacular manner, ranging from pitch black to brown and orange, all the way to the end of the fuselage and vane. It is a shame we can't share the noise with you, but rest ashured: it's loud !!!

Photo: Gert Trachez

Photo: Kris Christiaens

Above: The pilot of this Harrier II Plus is exiting his jet while deck crew is preparing to put the jet into it's parking spot. Notice the deck equipment that is used for this and that connects to the forward landing gear wheel.

Left: The deck handling equipment, chained to the deck, in close-up.

Duke Hawkins S001

Harrier Matador 19 is making a hard left hand turn and gives us a clear view of its belly. It is loaded with a Litening II pod on the centerline pylon, a pair of 2,000 lb droptanks on the inside pylons and a travel pod on the mid-pylon of the port wing. The aircraft is highly manoeuvrable and probably the most in it's element at low altitudes.

Juan Carlos Primero
AV-8B Harrier II Plus

Photo: Luis Diaz-Bedia Astor

Photo: Gert Trachez

Above: This pair of Harriers is making a break near the runway of Rota Air Base. Interesting to notice is that the Harrier on the right carries the 2,000 lb droptanks on the outer wet pylons, while the jet closest to the camera carries them on the inside pylons. Notice that the forward - cold - nozzles are painted in the fuselage colour, while the aft - hot - nozzles are left unpainted.

Left: Matador 17 is producing a mix of exhaust and vapor on the deck of the carrier.

Photo: Luis Diaz-Bedia Astor

Flying missions

The Harrier II Plus of the Spanish Navy are part of 9 Squadron, the only fixed wing unit in the Spanish Navy. Because of this, it's missions are very versatile, from Combat Air Patrols defending the Naval Task Group, to Close Air Support missions for ground troops or armed reconnaissance and attacks against land or sea targets with a wide assortment of weapons. The AV-8B was introduced into the 9th Squadron in 1987, but these were replaced some 10 years later by the AV-8B Harrier II Plus, with the more powerfull Pegasus Mk.107 engine. The unit has clocked over 50,000 flight hours.

Photo: Gert Trachez

Photo: Gert Trachez

Photo: Gert Trachez

Photo: Gert Trachez

Top: With the sun setting over the Atlantic Ocean, a pair of Harrier II Plus' parked behind the ship's super structure, are being prepared for a training mission.

Above and left: These close-ups give a good view of the three wing pylons. The two large ones are 'wet', meaning they can be loaded with external fuel tanks. In case of long missions, four 2,000 lb tanks can be carried.

Photo: Kris Christiaens

Above: A pilot is doing a walk-around of his jet before going on a training mission. He's checking the pitot tube and feels if the Forward Reaction Control Valve is clear. Notice the extended boarding step from the base of the air intake and the three boarding steps on the forward fuselage. Right: Four Matador IIs are chained to the flight deck, with the forward one halfway up the ski-ramp.

Juan Carlos Primero
AV-8B Harrier II Plus

Photo: Luis Díaz-Bedia Astor

Photo: Sergio Ruiz Gonzalez

9th Aircraft Squadron

The 9th Squadron consists of 24 officers (1 Commanding Officer, 20 other pilots and 3 maintenance officers, 67 NCOs and 81 Leading seamen and ratings. The photo above shows one of the aircraft flying at low level during a training mission. Notice the triple bomb dispencers on the middle pylons.

Right: Concentration is required before take off. Notice the name of the pilot underneath the canopy. Some of the dynamic air-to-air photos in this book are made by the same pilot - like the one on page 34!

Photo: Kris Christiaens

Right: I like this photo a lot; only with the Harrier it is possible to make a near static aerial photograph. This Harrier II Plus is hovering with its gear up. Notice the size of the large trailing edge flaps, vectoring the downward thrust coming from the hot engine nozzles. See the angle of the two fuselage fences.

Photo: Sergio Ruiz Gonzalez

Photo: Gert Trachez

Above: Chaff and flare dispensers are part of the defensive system of the Spanish Harriers - both on top and below on the aft fuselage, a total of 6 dispensers are located. Since the Harrier is often used in Close Air Support missions, these are vital.

Photo: Sergio Ruiz Gonzalez

Above: A Matador is transitioning from hovering to horizontal flight and is retracting its landing gear, while the large trailing edge flaps are still down. The light of the lower navigation light gives a red glow to the main landing gear. Notice the typical horizontal blade antenna under the nose.

Photo: Luis Diaz-Bedia Astor

A pair of Harriers is flying in close formation over the ocean back towards the ship. Notice the position of the nozzles and the closed bleed air doors on the air intake. The Spanish Navy has a long tradition using the VSTOL Harrier, which started with the AV-8A back in the days. The current Harrier is very much the better perfomer, thanks to the "big wing", developped by McDonnell Douglas. The fuselage is basiccaly the same though. This photo shows to good effect the differences in weathering between the two jets. Notice how the radomes are very different and how the Harrier in the lead has parts of the flaps and ailerons painted in a lighter shade of grey.

Photo: Gert Trachez

Juan Carlos Primero
AV-8B Harrier II Plus

Photo: Gert Trachez

Photo: Sergio Ruiz Gonzalez

Two great, but very different portraits of the Harrier II Plus: above is a jet about to touch down on the deck of the Juan Carlos I aircraft carrier, while the photo to the left is pure action, with a Harrier II Plus pulling up sharply, producing a lot of vapor and G's.

A Look around the flight deck

The deck of an aircraft carrier is an exciting place to visit. It is always buzzing with activity, Harriers taking off, helicopters landing and bringing equipment, deck crew securing jets to the deck and equipment being driven around. In this chapter, we give you a closer look at deck and everything that is going on on it.

Photo: Kris Christiaens

Juan Carlos Primero Flight Deck

Photo: Fuerzas Armadas Españolas

Above: The Juan Carlos I is making a sharp turn to port, while the deck is filled with 4 Sea King helicopters and 8 EAV-8B Harrier IIs, or Matador II, as they are known by the Fuerzas Armadas Españolas. Mid-island, the Spanish flag proudly flies.

Photo: Gert Trachez

Seen from the ship's island, the jump ramp is the most prominent part of the forward section of the flight deck. By using this ramp, the Harrier IIs are able to take off with a bigger load than if they were to take off vertically. The area ot the right of the ramp is used as a parking spot for helicopters or Harriers. In front of the large elevator is a smaller one to bring weapons or equipment on deck.

The flight deck of the Juan Carlos I is 201,90 meter long and 32 meter wide, with a distincive 12° ski -jump ramp in the front. For night operations, the deck can be lit up, as seen in this photo, with the flight axl centrally and blue lights on the port side of the deck. Notice all the tie-down points all over the deck and ship elevators. The entire deck has a surface of 5,440 square meters. There are 6 reinforced spots on the deck for mid-size or larger helicopters, with one for an Osprey or CH-53 Super Stallion. There are two large elevators - one in the back that is 13,30 meters by 11,20 meters, and another forward - starboard side of the island - 17 x 11,20 meters - with capacity for just over 27 tons.

Photo: Luis Diaz-Bedia Astor

Above: This photo shows the aft part of the flight deck, with crew parking the harriers before securing them to the deck.

Right: The elevator on the aft of the flight deck is 13,30 by 11,20 meters and is used for bringing Harriers or helicopters up from the hangar deck. This deck elevator is quite similar to the one of the aircraft carrier Principe de Asturias, the ship that preceded the Juan Carlos I.

Photo: Gert Trachez

Photo: Kris Christiaens

Left: Ordnance men - recognisable by their red vests - use the large elevator at the back of the deck to bring up an external fuel tank for a Harrier II Plus to the flight deck. It is transported on a little trolley around the deck. On page 15 you can see that it takes 3 of them to link it to the pylon. When the aircraft is completely filled up, it has a ferry range of about 3,300 km, but the combat radius of the jet is 556 km; that is, without refuelling in the air ...

The Spanish Navy has a long tradition flying the Harrier. It started operating the AV-8S, which is the Spanish version of the AV-8A back in 1976. It had 10 of them in service, but sold these to Thailand, when it decided to replace them with the first generation AV-8B Harrier II in 1983. The deliveries of the EAV-8B Harrier II Plus started in 1996. The jets were operated during Operation Deny Flight, which enforced the no-fly zone over Bosnia and Herzegovina in former Yugoslavia.

There are three types of carts that operate around the flight deck. Well, there is also a huge crane, which is mostly stowed in the aft part of the super structure, but, we'll have a closer look at that further in the book. These photos show the three I was talking about, with the one below left used specifically by the fire fighters on deck. When there's no flying, these vehicles are firmly secured to the deck by means of chains and wheel chocks that are stowed on the island - as you can see in the photo to the right.

Photo: Kris Christiaens

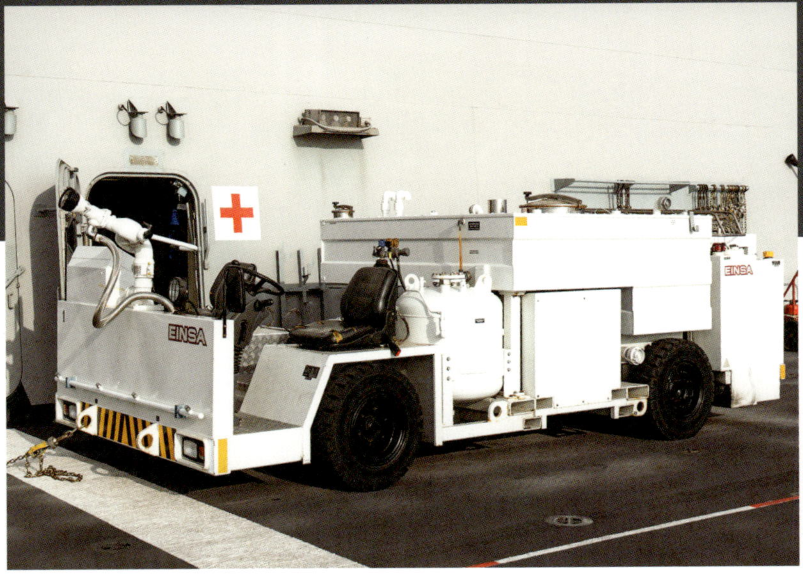

Photo: Kris Christiaens

Photo: Kris Christiaens

ARMADA

Juan Carlos Primero Flight Deck

So, what do you do when you have a fantastic photo like this available? You use it as a spread, right? The calm in this photo is completely opposite of the brutal noise that the Harriers make when they are hovering over the deck during landing procedures or when they throttle up for take off. Notice all the markings on the deck, which are painted white, red or yellow.

Photo: Kris Christiaens

Photo: Kris Christiaens

Photo: Kris Christiaens

Time to refuel the jet! This is the responsability of the deck crew wearing purple vests. The Harrier has a single refuelling point, located on the port side of the aircraft, immediately below the forward nozzle fairing. While refuelling the jet - in this case with the engine running - the in-flight refuelling probe is extended. The hose, through which the fuel is being pomped, is linked to a connection inside the ship's super structure, and can easily be rolled up again after refuelling. To the aft of the island, other connections can be found, such as distilled water, which is used by the Harrier to inject into the engine for emergency power. The filler cap for the water is located on top of the fuselage, next to the GPS antenna.

Photo: Kris Christiaens

Photo: Kris Christiaens

Helicopter Operations

The official designation of the Juan Carlos I is LHD - Landing Helicopter Dock - for which it is widely used. There is a large variety of helicopter types that operate from the carrier, such as the Chinook - seen in the photo to the right - but also Sea Kings, Cougars, Agusta-Bell AB-212 and in the near future the Airbus Helicopters NH-90. Even the small Hughes 369 helicopter of the 6th Naval Squadron can be operated from the ship, although these usually stay at Rota for pilot training. There are 6 reinforced spots on the deck for mid-size or larger helicopters, with one for a V-22 Osprey or a helicopter the size of a CH-53 Super Stallion. During helicopter operations, the deck crew has to be aware of the specifics of these helicopters, such as the downwash from the rotor blades, but the basic landing manoeuvres are quite similar to those of the Harriers. In this chapter, we show you some of the activities we witnessed during our stay.

Photo: Gert Trachez

Photo: Fuerzas Armadas Españolas

Photo: Gert Trachez

Juan Carlos Primero
Helicopter Operations

Photo: Kris Christiaens

The Sea King is one of the best known and trusted helicopters in the world, with over 1,300 of them built and many still in service. The Spanish Sea Kings are flown by the 5th Squadron, which was formed at Rota in 1966. Spain aquired 18 of them and initially they were tasked with anti-submarine missions, lateron expanding this for three of them to AEW - Airborne Early Warning - missions. Today, the Sea Kings are also used for troop carrying duties, which was the case when we visited the ship. Marines - some in training - has to exit the helicopters one by one in full equipment as fast as they could. Over and over again! The helicopters came in from Landing Platform Dock ships Galicia - L51 - and her sister ship Castilla - L52 - which participated in the excercise during our stay. The crew on the command deck in the photo above, ensured that the Juan Carlos I was in perfect position - with the nose in the wind - to receive the pair of helicopters. The Sea Kings are soon to be withdrawn from service, after a career spanning 6 (!) decades and will be replaced by NH-90 helicopters.

Photo: Kris Christiaens

Marines in full combat gear, including bullet proof vests, are climbing back into a Sea King helicopter, after they have exited it one by one for training purposes. Notice that one of them is having the back of her collegues during this manoeuvre. The Sea King has been in service with the Spanish Navy since 1966, and this was the seventh of the type to be delivered. Fun fact is that the first one, coded "501" is still in service. Notice the search pod fixed to the starboard side of the nose and the many rivets on the fuselage.

Sea King 507 was accompanied by Sea King 516 for the troop carrying training mission with the Marines. Standing very close to the helicopter, Kris and Gert can account for the noise and downwash produced by this loud pair. The Sea King is a big helicopter, with a length of 16.69 meter and a main rotor diameter of 19 meter. It is powered by a pair of General Electric T58-GE-10 turboshaft engines, producing each some 1,400 hp. Enough to transport in this case six fully armed and packed Marines at a speed of some 250 km/h!

Fast forward

Photo: Kris Christiaens

Photo: Gert Trachez

Left: The final Marine is getting into the cargo bay of the Sea King helicopter, while the winch operator is checking everything quickly for a speedy take off. Notice the green navigation light on the helicopter's sponson. The Spanish Navy's Sea Kings have an inflatable emergency float added outboard of the sponsons, to ensure an increased flotation whenever the helicopter has to make a landing on water. Notice in the photo above the green tinted upper windows for the flight crew.

Photo: Kris Christiaens

Photo: Gert Trachez

Aircraft handlers, recognisable by their yellow vests, are standing by while two Sea kings are on approach towards the Juan Carlos I. Looking ever so cool, they make sure the Sea Kings land exactly where they are supposed to and have wheel chock and chains at the ready, should they need to. The photos on the opposite page show one of the Sea Kings while manoeuvring over the deck. The Atlantic Ocean near the Bay of Dadiz is one of the busiest sea lanes there is, with ships going to and coming from the Mediterranean as can be seen in the background...

Photo: Gert Trachez

Photo: Kris Christiaens

Photo: Gert Trachez

Photo: Fuerzas Armadas Españolas

Left: An Agusta-Bell AB 212+ - affectionally known as 'Huey' - is being lowered on the ship's forward elevator, while a Sea King is parked next to the jump ramp. The Spanish Navy has been operating this helicopter type since 1974 and has 7 of them in service. The Juan Carlos I has two deck elevators, one in front of the ship's island and another at the very end of the deck. The Hueys are operated by 3 Squadron and perform anti-surface warfare, search and rescue, transport and logistical missions. And even though the type has already had a long career, it is sure to remain operational in the Spanish Navy for at least another 15 years!

Photo: Kris Christiaens

Right: A Harrier pilot with over 1500 flying hours on the type, is watching a Cougar helicopter land on the flight deck from his seat in the command room. Notice that while doing so, the helicopter is being filmed from different angles, while an eye can be kept on the bow of the ship and even the hangar deck, although it seems to be quite empty. The screen to the right shows the position of the Juan Carlos I in the Bay of Cadiz, in a north-westerly heading.

o: Fuerzas Armadas Españolas

A Eurocopter AS-532UL Cougar of the Fuerzas Aeromóviles del Ejército de Tierra - the Spanish Army - is about to land on the deck.The helicopter is powered by a pair of Turbomeca Makila 1A1 turoshaft engines and can carry a load of nearly 4.5 tons! The helicopter is part of the 2nd Emergency Helicopter Battalion, based at Bétera, near Valencia. Spain's Army also operates the Eurocopter Tiger attack helicopter and the Chinook transport helicopter.

Photo: Gert Trachez

Photo: Gert Trachez

Photo: Gert Trachez

These photos show an Agusta-Bell AB-212 helicopter in approach and briefly on the deck of the Juan Carlos I. The Spanish Navy has seven of the type in its inventory since 1974 and all have received an extensive update over the last years, in order to exteded their operational life by at least 15 years. The update provided the helicopters with new equipment, such as night vision systems, radar and self-defense mechanisms. Notice how the engine exhausts stain the aft part of the fuselage!

Juan Carlos Primero
Helicopter Operations

Photo: Gert Trachez

Duke Hawkins 5001

Photo: Kris Christiaens

Photo: Kris Christiaens

Above and left: Helicopter operations on the deck require close collaboration between many of the deck crew. The helicopter crew waits for the signals from the plane handlers - dressed in blue - that the chains and wheel chocks are cleared from the helicopter. They are under the direction of the yellow shirted aircraft handler, who is responsable for moving aircraft around the flight deck. All the time the engines are running, firemen are on stand-by for any eventually.

Opposite page: International exercises and collaborations are important to ensure that when the time comes for allies have to work together, it all goes fluently. This photo shows a US Marines V-22 Osprey on the forward deck of the Juan Carlos I during one such exercise, parked in front of a duo of Matadors.

Amphibious Operations

Photo: Kris Christiaens

The aft part of the ship has a floodable area of 69,30 meter long ans 16,8 meter wide, giving room for 4 LCM-1E landing crafts. With these boats, troops, military vehicles and equipment can be brought on land during amphibious assaults. It can also be used to launch an LCAC - Landing Craft Air Cushion. During our visit, excercises were held with LCM-1E's, giving us the possibility to show you these spectacular photos!

Photo: Kris Christiaens

Photo: Kris Christiaens

The LCM-1E is just over 23 meter long and 6,4 meter wide, with a capacity to be loaded with a main battle tank, 2 Mowag Piranha IIIC armoured fighting vehicles or up to 6 light tactical vehicles. Loaded only with troops, it gives room to 170 fully equipped soldiers. The photo above shows an LCM-1E loaded with an ambulance, a Piranha IIIC and about a dozen troops. These landing crafts have a range of 350 km and a speed of 25 km/h when fully loaded, giving the troops an enormous flexibility and speed. They have a stern gate, as can be seen in the photo above, allowing the vehicles to be loaded and unloaded withing the ship.

Left: A Mowag Piranha IIIC is being driven back to the front of the ship after a training mission.

Photo: Kris Christiaens

Left: This is the aft part of the Deck dock with the floodable area actually being lowered; notice the stern door of the ship going down. The narrow ramp in the middle is just wide enough for one person to check if everything is going the way it should. On each side of the ramp, two LCM-1E landing craft can be positioned and loaded. The floodable area is 69,30 meter long and 16,80 meter wide. Notice the structure of the side walls and ceiling.

Right: The crew of this Mowag Piranha IIIC 8x8 is preparing to get back to the ship and drive off the landing craft, into the heavy vehicle garage, located in front of the deck dock. The Spanish Navy Marines has a total of 39 of these armoured vehicles, in 3 different versions. The Piranha has a length of 7,30 meter and can reach speeds of up to 100 km/h. It has a 400 hp engine with a 7-speed automatic transmission. The armoured vehicles have protection against ballistic threats and mines and are used for a wide variety of missions, such as Recovery & Reconnaissance, ambulance, as a mobile command post, and more. The all-wheel drive and modern independent wheel suspension give the Marines maximum mobility, even in difficult terrain.

Photo: Kris Christiae

Photo: Kris Christiaens

Photo: Gert Trachez

Above: Forward of the floodable area, a 1,480 square meters garage for heavy vehicles is located. Here, trucks, armoured vehicles, jeeps, and even tanks can be stored. It is even possible to store up to 46 Leopard tanks and considering that they weigh a hefty 62 tons a piece, that is quite impressive!

Left: A well filled LCM-1E landing craft is steaming towards the stern of the ship, into the floodable area located in the dock deck.

Photo: Kris Christiaens

Above: The Juan Carlos I is being loaded, prior to the excercise. Notice all the ropes with which the ship is moored.

Right: There are two side access doors from the deck dock towards the harbor dock for boarding vehicles - in this case a VAMTAC ST5 BN 3, a four-wheel drive military vehicle comparable to the Humvee. Crew and Marines enter the ship by means of an access door next to it.

Photo: Gert Trachez

Right: With the LCM-1E landing craft safely secured to the side walls of the deck dock, the Marines prepare to drive the vehicles into the garage in front of it. In the days and weeks following the 2010 earthquake in Haiti, these landing crafts were used to bring relief personnel and emergency equipment directly to the island's beaches. This proved the flexibility of the forces, since the Haitian ports were either destroyed by the earthquake or completely congested by other ships. The LCM-1E is mainly used out of the Juan Carlos I, but can also operate from the two Galicia-class landing platform dock ships - see page 79.

Photo: Gert Trachez

Photo: Kris Christiaens

Photo: Gert Trachez

Photo: Gert Trachez

These photos show the 1,480 square meters large garage for heavy vehicles, situated in front of the floodable area. When the LCM-1Es are docked inside the ship - see opposite page - 16 tons of leverage is needed inside the garage. Notice the three long lines of military trucks, armoured vehicles, ambulances and four-wheel drive military vehicles being neatly parked. and secured to the deck.

Photo: Kris Christiaens

Photo: Kris Christiaens

The Juan Carlos I is loaded with a lot of fuel during operations; About 500 tons of DFM fuel is available for the landing forces and boats. Reservoirs inside the ship also hold 800 tons of JP-5 fuel for the Harrier II Plus and helicopters, operating from the ship. The quantity of fuel that is loaded for the ship itself amounts to 1,649 tons! This gives the ship a maximum range of 9,000 nautical miles or 17,000 km. Another impressive statistic of the Juan Carlos I is this: there is a capacity of holding 479,000 liters of drinking water on board. Thirsty, anyone?

Intellian
AFFF
4
EINSA
EINSA

Photo: Kris Christiaens

Photo: Kris Christiaens

The Juan Carlos I in close-up

It is a fascinating thing to be aboard an aircraft carrier such as the Juan Carlos I, especially when you have the possibility to get a closer look at the different parts of the ship. We already took a look around the flight deck, but in this chapter, we give a closer look at the super structure and the interior of the ship. It shows the surprising flexibility of the ship, which has four specific roles: Strategic projection, Amphibious Operations, being an aircraft carrier and Military Operations other than War. Fortunately, the Spanish flagship is often used for the latter. The Juan Carlos I has four main decks and seven others. The four main decks are the flight deck, which is 201,90 meter long and 32 meter wide, with the distincive 12° ski -jump ramp ; the Hangar and garage deck for light vehicles - here aircraft, helicopters and small vehicles are stored ; the Hability deck, where most accommodations for the crew are located, such as hospital facilities, dining rooms, recreational rooms, ... ; and finally the deck for the heavy vehicles and the floodable area in the aft part of the deck, where the LCM's can be launched from. So, lets take a closer look!

Photo: Gert Trachez

Photo: Kris Christiaens

A lot can be seen on the deck and the superstructure of the ship. At the far end of the superstructure, behind the stern post, the aircraft approach radar Aries-PAR can be found, assisting the pilots to land on the flight deck, even during less than ideal weather conditions. The system consists of two antennas: one for azimuth and another for elevation. The photo to the left shows the system in detail. Notice the round multi-camera system on the railing aft of the approach radar and the green lights in the photo to the right.

Photo: Kris Christiaens

A little more info on the aft mast of the super structure: here, the Air Search Radar Indra Aries-SAAS - Surface and Air Surveillance is located, which is designed to detect airborne targets and conduct tasks control aircraft. This Aries-SAAS also collects radar capabilities from Aries-NAV, the Surface Search and Navigation Radar, which is located in the formast under the Lanza-N radar.
Right: The forward command post seen from on top of the island.

Photo: Kris Christiaens

Photo: Gert Trachez

Photo: Kris Christiaens

Photo: Gert Trachez

Photo: Gert Trachez

Above: In the middle of the super structure of the ship, a mast with radar and communication equipment is located. Notice all the wires running from it.

Above right: This structure can be found immediately aft of the super structure.

Right: In front of the island, a large crane is located next to the big elevator, on the starboard side of the ship. It is capable of moving up to 20 tons around or from the dock onto the flight deck.

Photo: Kris Christiaens

Right: During the excercise that was held in the Gulf of Cadiz during our visit, the Juan Carlos I was joined by the Galicia - L51 - and her sister ship Castilla - L52 - in the back. Both are Landing Platform Dock ships that have been active in the Spanish fleet for some 20 years. They are 160 meters long and have a flight deck for two helicopters - see the pair of Sea Kings on the Castilla. These ships have been used during many humanitarian missions, such as relief missions in Haiti after the 2010 earthquake. Both ships, like the Juan Carlos I, have Rota as their home port.

Photo: Gert Trachez

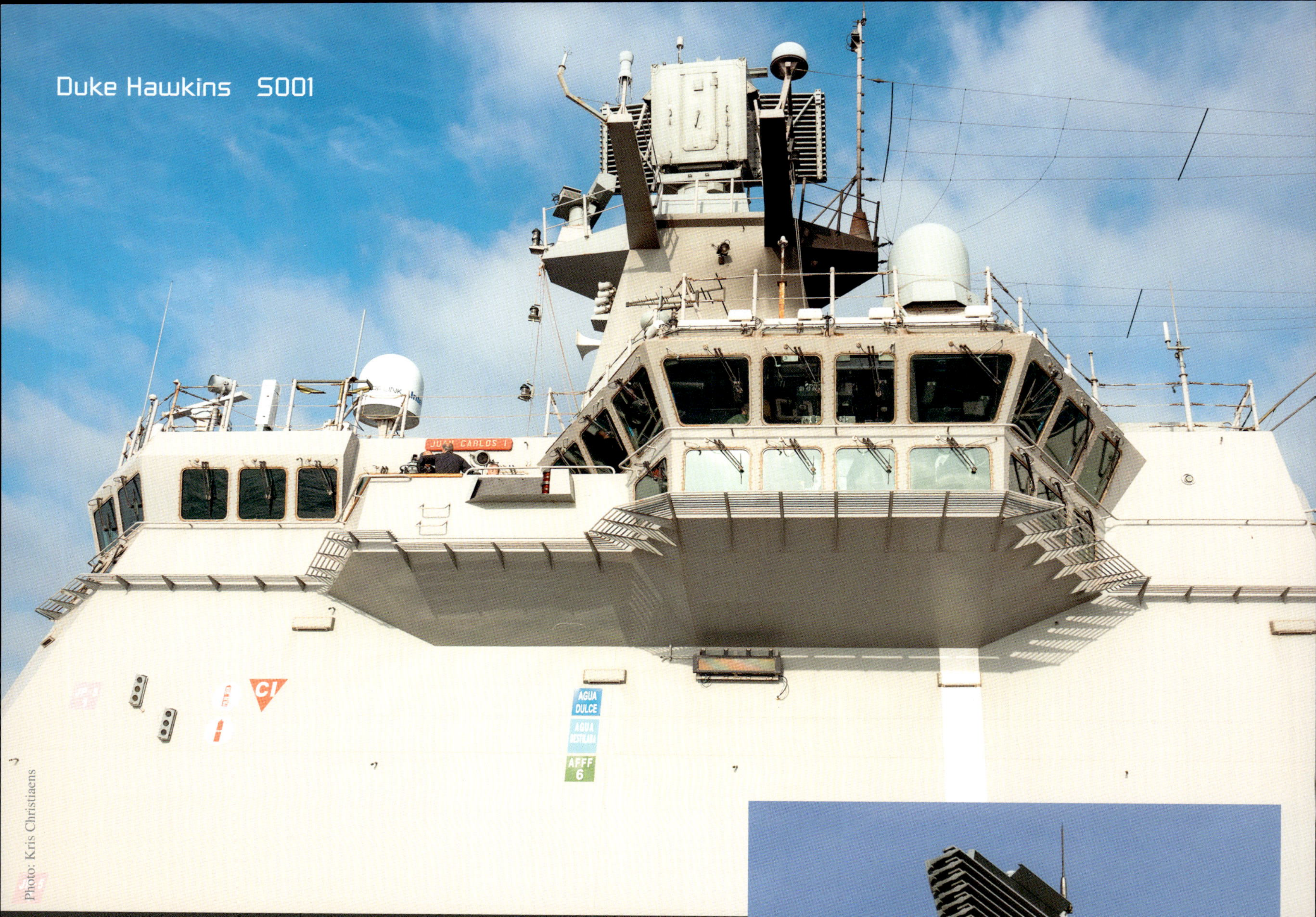

Photo: Kris Christiaens

Above: this photo shows the forward section of the super structure of the Juan Carlos I, with the command post and bridge of the ship. The ship is filled with many modern sensors and systems, like the Air Radar, which is based on Indra Lanza-N, a navalised versions of the radar used by the Spanish Air Force. Altough the actual size of the antenna is smaller than previous versions, it is extremely performant and has a coverage of 180 nautical miles. The front mast, on top of the super structure also holds the Surface Search and Navigation Radar. Over the bridge, a Northrop Grumman Sperry Marine VisionMaster FT radar is installed for navigation radar capabilities. The ship is equipped with an IFF system - Identification Friend or Foe, an Optronics Surveillance System and two Electronic Warfare systems: the Indra Rigel band radar and the Indra Regulus communications system.

Photo: Kris Christiaens

Right and below: In the aft part of the super structure of the Juan Carlos I, a large crane is located. Notice that next to it, connections for fresh and distilled water are located. The latter is used by the Harriers II Plus' to inject into the engine's combustion chamber to obtain temporarily more thrust. The water makes sure the temperature of the compressor blades is kept down in high rpm.

Photo: Kris Christiaens

Photo: Kris Christiaens

The Juan Carlos I is equipped with SCOMBA - Sistema de COMbate de Buques de la Armada, which is a combat system developped in Spain that drives video signals from radar, FLIR - Forward Looking Infra Red - and CCTV systems to consoles located in the OPS Room and CTA. SCOMBA is used on most of the ships of the Spanish Navy, thus homogenising the different units.

Photo: Gert Trachez

Above: This photo gives a good view of the entire port side of the Juan Carlos I, with the 12 degree ski-jump ramp and the super structure. Notice where the ship's large ropes are connected. See where the fast zodiac is located and the forward guns for protecting the ship?

Below: A fast Zodiac, which is located in an opening, halfway the ship, is being lowered during an excercise. These boats can be used for quick interceptions or rescues.

Photo: Kris Christiaens

Photo: Gert Trachez

Photo: Gert Trachez

Photo: Kris Christiaens

The Ship's hangar

Above: This photo shows the hangar deck located immediately below the flight deck. This continuous - and honestly very impressive - deck provides room for the aircraft and helicopters operating from the ship. There is room for 19 Harrier II Plus or up to 30 mid-size helicopters. Even if 10 large CH-47 Chinooks are parked in the hangar, there is still room for 12 other helicopters and 10 Harriers. Light vehicles that are used on the deck can be stowed in the hangar as well. Notice the monorail crane, capable of handling loads of up to 1 ton.
Right: Racks on the side walls of the hangar are used to store the large external fuel tanks of the Harriers.

Photo: Kris Christiaens

Right: A pair of Harrier II Plus' and a Sea King helicopter with folded rotor blades are parked and secured in the hangar deck. Notice the external fuel tanks stored in racks placed on the hangar's side walls. The probe antennas on either side of the forward fuselage have been covered for protection.

Photo: Luis Díaz-Bedia Astor

Below: Halfway on the port side wall, a command post oversees the entire hangar deck. These two photos show the command post from both the outside and the inside.

Photo: Kris Christiaens

Photo: Kris Christiaens

Photo: Kris Christiaens

These photos show the control room for the ship's engines. The propulsion of the carrier is fully electric and consists of a gas turbine CM-2500, generating 19,750 hp and two Navantia-MAN 3/40 diesel generators which provide for the electricity of the vessel and power the bow thrusters. To move the ship, two pods near the stern are used, each with two three-bladed propellers. These pods are highly effective and make the ship very manoeuvrable, because they can rotate 360 degrees.

Photo: Kris Christiaens

Photo: Gert Trachez

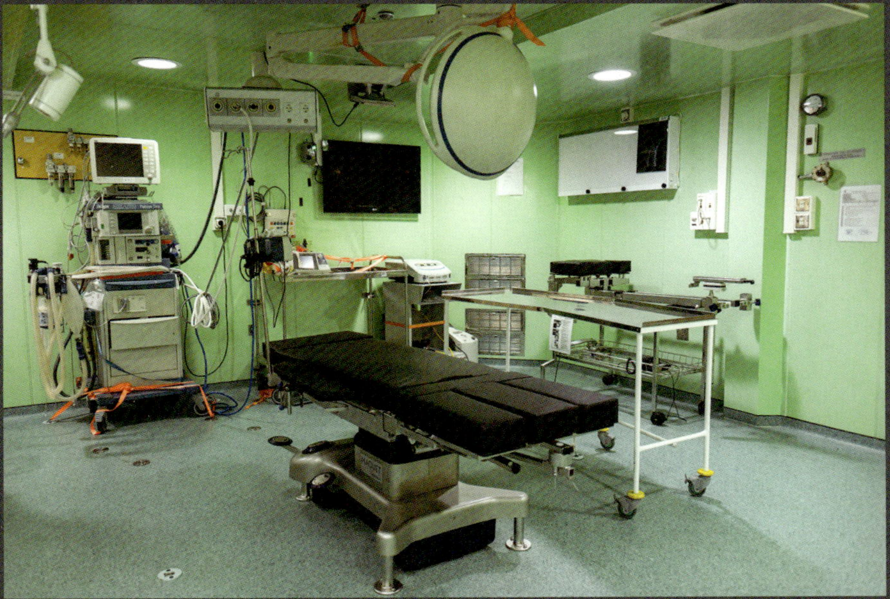

Photo: Kris Christiaens

The Juan Carlos I is ideal for use in humanitarian missions and as such is fully equipped. There is a casualty examination area with six stretchers, an isolation ward for 4 patients, an X-ray room, pharmacy, dentist's office and two full surgery rooms - photo above.

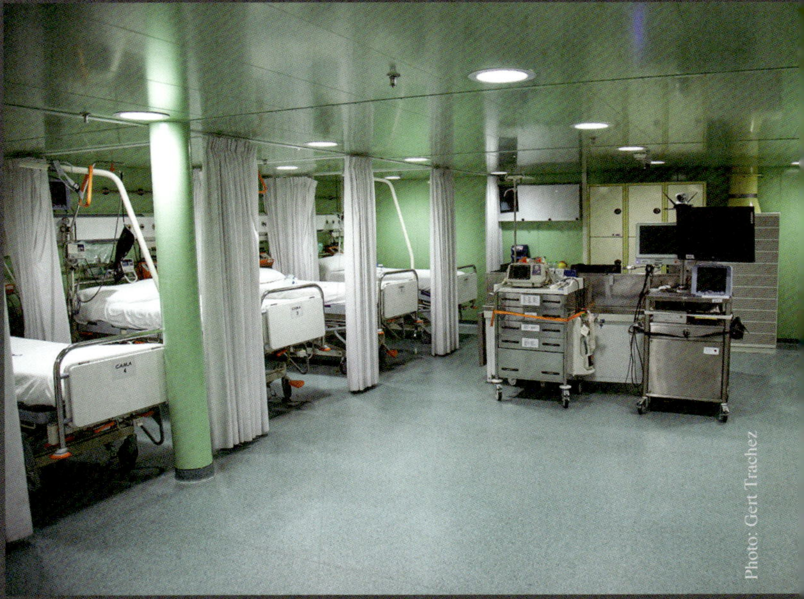

Photo: Gert Trachez

Above: This photo shows the Intesive Care unit on board the Juan Carlos I, which has room for 8 patients. Next to this, the ship has it's own laboratory and even a sterilisation room.

Photo: Gert Trachez

Above: This photo shows the briefing room that is used by pilots, flight crew and commanders to go over the missions or excercises.

Photo: Kris Christiaens

One of the 4 main decks of the ship is the Habitability deck, where most of the crew accommodations, kitchens, dining rooms and recreational rooms are located. As is this gym.

Photo: Kris Christiaens

Photo: Gert Trachez

Photo: Kris Christiaens

Above: This photo shows the after deck of the Juan Carlos, with the big elevator and the flight deck at the top. Notice the huge ropes that are used when the ship is moored at the docks.

Above right: These tubes are of the Mk-36 SRBOC countermeasures system installed on the ship. There 6 of these, each with 6 tubes. Two are on the stern of the ship, two on the bow and two more on each tack.

Right: These massive chains are of the ship's anchor. For a ship the size of the Juan Carlos I, huge anchors and chains are needed, as well as powerful engines to bring the anchors back up!

Photo: Kris Christiaens

These two photos give you an idea of the size of the large elevator at the back of the ship and the engine and equipment necessary to operate it.

The photo above shows the aircraft hangar, immediately below the flight deck, with in the middle below the equipment. Next to the two large elevators, the Juan Carlos I has a light load lift of 20 tons between decks 1 and 4. A 2 ton lift is used to bring ammunition on deck and additional lifts are used for the hospital, for food and VIPs.

Protecting the Ship

The main protection for the Juan Carlos I are of course the Harriers that operate from the ship, but there is also a small component on the ship itself, next to the countermeasures with which it is equipped. The armament is limited to 4 Oerlikon 20 mm guns and four 12,7 mm Browning machine guns. The ship also provides room for a future weapons defense system and an anti-torpedo system. During our visit, a firing excercise was held, which showed the impressive power of the 20 mm guns. And again: loud ! The Oerlikon gun has it's origins in a German design from World War I, but even the current version is still very much one of which you don't want to be on the receiving end...

Photo: Gert Trachez

The guns installed on the Juan Carlos I aren't often used, except to fire warning shots at small boats apporaching the ship without permission. The ship's radars, sensors and FLIR make sure that any surface contact is noticed well in advance. And if an armed helicopter or a Harrier II Plus is used to intervene, chances are the other vessel will comply quickly to instructions given!

Photo: Gert Trachez

Photo: Kris Christiaens

Photo: Kris Christiaens

Home base at Rota

Photo: Luis Diaz-Bedia Astor

On land, the home base of the aircraft and helicopters that operate from the Juan Carlos I, such as the Harriers, Sea Kings, or Seahawks is Rota, in the southern part of Spain near the port of Cadiz. The base is shared with American forces, who called it Naval Station Rota, housing US Navy, US Marine Corps and US Air Force personnel. These pages show some of the activity going on at Rota and were taken by our duo Kris and Gert, as well as Antonio Mayandia and Laurent Heyligen, who went on an extensive base visit in the spring of 2018.

One of the units based at Rota is 10 Squadron, which was formed in 1988. It operates the Sikorsky SH-60B and SH-60F Seahawk helicopter, which is used for many different missions. In all, 12 Seahawks were purchased in two batches of 6 and are used for anti-submarine missions, Search and Rescue, Medical Evacuation, Vertical Replenishments and Naval Surface Fire Support.

Photo: Laurent Heyligen

Photo: Laurent Heyligen

Depending on the missions, the Seahawks can be equipped with different systems, like a FLIR - Forward Looking Infra-Red - IFF - Identification Friend or Foe or ESM - Electronic Support Measures. It can be loaded with different kinds of weapons, such as the Hellfire missile for short range targets or the AGM119 Penguin anti-ship missile, which can be effective at a range of up to 20 nautical miles.

Photo:Sergio Ruiz Gonzalez

The photo above shows the much higher position of the pilot in the back of the two-seat Harrier. One of the typical features of the two-seat version, is the larger vertical tail. Notice the two yaw vanes, one for each of the crew.

Photo: Laurent Heyligen

Photo: Laurent Heyligen

This two-seat Harrier II is undergoing maintenance at Rota. An engineer is working on the connections between the wing and fuselage. In order to work on the engine, the entire top wing has to be removed, hence the work on the connections, each time the wing has to be removed or reconnected.

Photo: Laurent Heyligen

This pair of Sea Kings is parked on the ramp of Rota Naval Air Base, with the one in the back undergoing some maintenance on the engines. The Sea Kings have been in service for a long time and are nearing the end of their career with 5 Squadron.

Photo: Laurent Heyligen

This Sea King is having it's engine reviewed. The filters in front of the General Electric T58-GE-10 turboshaft engines are removed and all of the 4 large engine covers are open. See the engineer sitting on the forward port engine door? Notice that this is actually the same machine as the one on page 56, bringing some Marines on the deck of the Juan Carlos I

Right: This SH-60 Seahawk of 10 Squadron is parked inside the hangar and has it's main rotor blades folded back. I think the Seahawk is such a great looking helicopter that doesn't age at all!

Below: The Harrier II Plus is a complex aircraft to fly. On top of the usual flying, the pilot has to master the aircraft when it is hovering or flying at extremely low speeds. This is why an extensive training on the two-seat version is really important.

Photo: Laurent Heyligen

Photo:Sergio Ruiz Gonzalez

oto: Laurent Heyligen

Above: An Agusta-Bell AB-212 helicopter is hovering over it's parking spot at Rota. It has been part of the 3rd Squadron ever since 1974 and has seen extensive updates since, including night vision systems and a self-defense mechanism.

Right: Now this is a such a great shot of a Matador II about to land on the ramp at Rota. I like this photo, because you can almost feel the heat and downwash produced by the Pegasus Mk.107 engine. The trailing edge flaps, gear and Lift Improvement Device immediately aft of the nose wheel are all down. This is when the pilot has to show that he is in total control of his jet; although it probably is even harder to land the Harrier II on the deck of an aircraft carrier moving into the wind at speeds of 20 knots.

Photo:Sergio Ruiz González

Duke Hawkins S001

Photo:Sergio Ruiz Gonzalez

Low level: that's where the Harrier II Plus is at his best! It is carrying a GAU-12U Equaliser gun underneath the fuselage instead of the fuselage fences. The Harrier packs a serious punch and can be loaded with up to 6 tons of ordnance, from air-to-air to air-to-ground or sea weapons. Notice the target pod on the starboard inboard pylon.

Photo: Laurent Heyligen

Another naval squadron based at Rota is 6 Escadrilla, operating the Hughes 369. These helicopters, in their initial role, operated off destroyers and were equipped with floats. They could also be loaded with torpedoes. Today, the unit is mostly a training squadron for pilots that hope eventually to transition to the Sea King, Seahawk and in the future the NH-90 helicptor, which will replace the aging Sea King. The Spanish Navy has ordered 7 of the type.

Right: A closer look at the cockpit of the Hughes 369, of which the squadron operates 9. Next to pilot training, the helicopters are also used for Special Operations, as a Sniper platform or even for Forward Air Control. The Hughes 369 can also be operated from the ship, for maritime surveillance, medical evacuation or other missions.

Photo: Laurent Heyligen

Maintenance at Rota

No Harrier is getting airborne if it didn't pass the maintenance checks. Because of the VSTOL capability of the aircraft, the jet has some specific needs, especially when it comes to the Pegasus Mk.107 engine and the mechanism for the nozzles. Whenever maintenance is needed on the engine, or when it has to be changed, the entire wing has to be removed to get access to it. This isn't the easiest procedure, with the jet having to be placed on jacks, access doors having to be removed and a crane installed to remove the wing, which then has to be placed on a cradle. After this, the entire fuselage has to be canted downwards, the nozzles have to be removed and the engine can be removed. There's a lot of activity going on in the maintenance hangar at Rota and this chapter not only gives you a look inside of it, but it is also a bit of a tribute to all men and women taking care of the formidable fighter jet.

The photo to the right shows a Harrier II Plus on jacks in the maintenance hangar, which has a typical blue floor. Notice the extended landing gear, open avionics access underneath the nose, open circuitbraker panel underneath the windshield and the removed engine nozzles. Also notice the small open panels immediately aft of the radome; these have to be in this position in order to open the radome and fold it to starboard.

Photo: Kris Christiaens

Photo: Laurent Heyligen

Above: This Harrier II has been placed on jacks inside the Rota maintenance hangar, recognisable by it's typical blue floor. The wing has been placed back on the fuselage, after engine maintenance - an engineer is checking the wing-fuselage connections. Notice the retracted landing gear and the nose-down position of the aircraft. A pretty cool photo by Laurent Heyligen!

Photo: Antonio Mayandia

Above: Two pair of fuselage fences have been removed and stored in the maintenance hangar in Rota. These fences, fixed to the belly of the Harriers ensure stability during flight.

Photo: Antonio Mayandia

Above: The Harrier II Plus is equipped with an APG-65 radar, forcing the designers to reposition the Forward looking Infra-Red into a fairing, placed on top of the nose, in front of the windscreen.

Photo: Gert Trachez

Photo: Kris Christiaens

The large square panels on both sides of the nose give access to circuit brakers for the instruments in the cockpit. To make sure none of the screws are lost, they are held in a plastic bag fixed on the panel. The smaller panel underneath the ejection seat warning stencil pictures the throttle linkages and the pipe feeding the Environmental Control System, which provides air for the cockpit, thermal control, cabin pressure, avionics cooling and fire suppression. Notice in the photo above, the handle in front of the air intake cover, which opens the forward nose gear doors.

Left: The lower panel, aft of the air data probe cover, gives access to the Air Data Computer and is kept open with a single strut.

Photo: Antonio Mayandia

Left: This interesting photo by Antonio Mayandia shows the wing removed from the aircraft and placed on a special cradle. It is interesting to see that the wing pylons don't have to be removed in order to remove the wing from the fuselage.

Below: This Harrier II Plus is nearly ready to resume operational missions. Notice that the jet is carrying its external fuel tanks on the middle pylon. The forward jet nozzles are painted in the fuselage colour and are 'cold', while the aft ones are the 'hot' ones, blasting hot exhaust from the Pegasus engine. All 4 nozzles operate simultaniously by means of the Single Air Motor Servo Unit, in the cockpit.

Photo: Laurent Heyligen

Photo: Kris Christiaens

Above: Another pair of Matador IIs in Rota's maintenance hanger. The one in the front has its target pod on the centreline pylon, while the one in the back had his removed. An engine inspection panel on top of the aircraft is open.
Below: This photo shows the location of the engine inspection panel, next to the 100% Leading Edge Root Extension.
Right: A close-up of the SJU-4 ejection seat of the Harrier II Plus. Notice the yellow handle to the right of the seat. When this is placed in the up-position in the aircraft, the seat is armed.

Photo: Antonio Mayandia

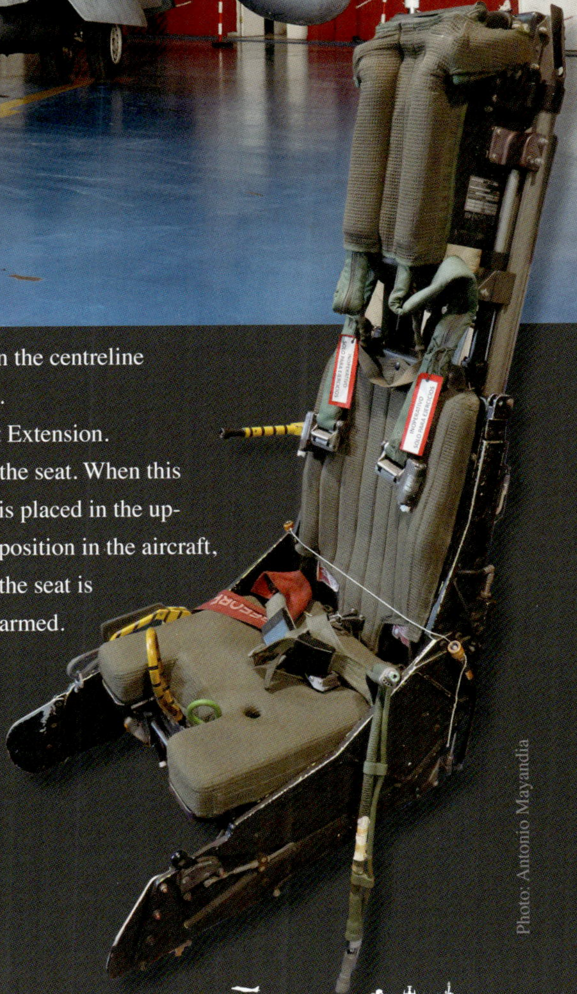

Photo: Antonio Mayandia

Photo: Gert Trachez

To end this first book in the new series, I picked two photos of a sunset on board of the Juan Carlos I, sailing across the Atlantic Ocean. The ship and especially the Harriers operating from it are simply impressive. Let's hope the latter will remain operational for quite some time, it is always fantastic to see a Harrier transition from hovering to high speed manoeuvres. We are extremely grateful that the Spanish Navy invited us to stay on the ship and I hope that we did a good job presenting it in this book. It was a privilege to do so!

Photo: Gert Trachez